KENAI

ALASKA'S KENAI PENINSULA

Begich-Boggs Visitor Center, Portage.

Front Cover: Aialik Glacier is one of seven tidewater glaciers in Kenai Fjords National Park.

Front Cover Inset: The tufted puffin makes its home along the Kenai coastline.

Inside Front Cover-1: McCarty Fjord, Kenai Fjords National Park.

Pages 2-3: A winter sunrise over Kachemak Bay illuminates the city of Homer.

Back Cover: A playful sea otter feasts on a snow crab leg.

PHOTO CREDITS

Alaska State Library: 27. Anchorage Museum: 37. Frank Balthis: 15, 39, 43, 46 top. Norma Wolf Dudiak: 16 top, 28, 29, 32 bottom, 40, 41 right. Laura Greffenius: Front cover inset, 18. David Kenagy: 16 bottom, 23 top, 30 bottom, 35 top right, 41 left, 42, 47. Chlaus Lötscher: 2-3, 6-7, 10, 17, 24, 30 top, 31, 33, 35 top left, 35 bottom, 36, 44, 46 bottom, 48. Steve McCutcheon: 8, 34. Joseph Meehan: Front cover, inside front cover-1, 21, 25. Sharie Methven: 12, 13, 38. Bob Moore: 45. Jim Pfeiffenberger: 14, 19 bottom. Susan Pfeiffenberger: 20. Bud Rice: 26. Ron Sanford: 4-5, 9, 11, 19 top, 23 middle and bottom, 32 top. Tom Walker: 22, back cover.

Editor: Angela Tripp
Art Director: Joanne Station
Editorial Consultant: Page Spencer
Editorial Assistant: Karrie Hyatt
Writers:
Jim Pfeiffenberger
Page Spencer, Norma Wolf Dudiak, Peter Fitzmaurice
Diana Thomas, Lisa Trujillo, Bob Moore

Albion Publishing Group
924 Anacapa St., Suite 3A
Santa Barbara, CA 93101
(805) 963-6004
Lorie Bacon, Publisher

© 1993 by Albion Publishing Group
All rights reserved. Published 1993
Printed in Hong Kong through Asiaprint, Ltd. USA
ISBN 1-880352-32-X

ACKNOWLEDGMENTS

We would like to acknowledge and thank the following for their assistance and contribution to this book. The help of these individuals and groups has been invaluable: Frankie Barker, Poppy Benson, Anne Castellina, Mark Franklin, Maria Gillette, the staff at Kenai Fjords National Park, Martha Massey, Mariah Charters, Jack Sinclair, and Candace Ward.

CONTENTS

INTRODUCTION

THE KENAI is a dynamic land—a land of natural richness, of singular beauty, of continual change. With all it offers, the Kenai Peninsula is more than just "Alaska's Playground." It is home to a wide variety of wildlife and humankind alike—from the gregarious puffin to the elusive bear, from the Native people to the more recent homesteaders. The inhabitants of the Kenai Peninsula live in a delicate ecosystem that moves with the rhythms of seasonal change, geologic phenomena, and human influence.

The Kenai is a land apart, separated from the Alaskan mainland by Cook Inlet and Prince William Sound but for a narrow thread of rock and ice. Were it not for this barely present isthmus, the Kenai would relinquish its tie to the Alaskan mainland. The unique and varied features of the land today are the work of ice and tectonics. The Kenai's coastal mountains have balanced precariously for millions of years on the junction of the North American and the Pacific plates. And for over 200,000 years glacial ice and the ocean have played chase with each other, surging up and back along Cook Inlet and the Kenai lowlands, leaving huge chunks of ice that melted into brilliantly hued lakes.

A young boy makes his way home through a snowstorm.

Glacial epochs are mirrored by annual seasonal cycles. Each spring, the mountains throw off their blankets of snow to reveal new leaves and wildflower meadows. The lakes and marshes are freed of winter ice, providing a welcoming place for migrating waterfowl to rest and raise their young. After a winter-long snooze, the bears emerge in early spring with tiny cubs, ready to explore a new summer world. Along stretches of rocky coast, sea lions give birth to new pups. In late summer, translucent green rivers turn gray with silt from melting glaciers and become homing highways for salmon returning to spawn. The salmon become food for prowling bears who must build enough fat reserves to see them through their winter hibernation.

In fall, the alpine tundra blazes with scarlet and yellow leaves, and the bears finish off their feast of blueberries before retreating to hidden dens for the winter. Early snow frosts the towering peaks, then swoops down mountain shoulders and into the lowlands, chasing half-grown swans and ducks in scattering Vs through the passes. Hares and ptarmigan turn white to hide in the winter landscape, leaving tracks of their lives woven through the tops of willows buried deep in the snow. Storms roar in from the Aleutian Islands, and once again the winds drift snow over the bear dens.

This rich cycle of seasons also nurtured the early human inhabitants of the Kenai Peninsula. The Dena'ina Indians and Chugach Eskimo lived near the rivers and coast for over a thousand years, finding food, shelter, and transportation from the animals and vegetation of the land and sea. Russian fur traders arrived in the late 1700s and established posts in what are today the city of Kenai and the village of Ninilchik, and near present-day Seward. The Russians were followed by English explorers, gold seekers, railroad construction workers, military forces, homesteaders, oil-field workers, and more Russians.

Today, the Kenai hosts a multitude of visitors who come to enjoy the unparalleled scenery and recreational opportunities. Whether you travel by car or motor home, train, tour boat, fishing skiff, white-water raft, canoe, sea kayak, skis, snowmobile, floatplane, or your own two feet, you will see some of the most amazing country on earth.

You are invited to slow down long enough to listen to the sound of trickling mountain streams and crashing ocean waves; to watch bears catching salmon in the rivers; to smell the fragrant wildflowers; to feast on ripe berries and fresh crab; to listen to the loons crying beneath the auroral curtains; to watch the sun circling above the mountains; to smell the aroma of your campfire smoke as it drifts into the spruce boughs overhead; to let snowflakes land in your hair; and yes, even to swat a few mosquitoes. Treat this powerful yet fragile place with care and respect. Get to know this land called the Kenai—and carry away memories for a lifetime.

WELCOME.

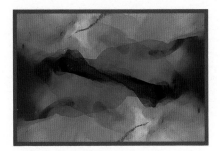

CHAPTER 1

EASTERN PENINSULA

The Kenai Peninsula is barely a peninsula at all. Ten thousand years ago, this rugged land was completely buried under snow and ice. Only the highest mountaintops showed through like jagged islands in a smooth, frozen sea. As mammoth glaciers carved their way down toward bedrock, cutting away at the land, they very nearly made an island of the Kenai Peninsula. But the glaciers retreated before the job was done. Today, a strip of mountainous land just twelve miles wide separates the waters of Turnagain Arm from those of Prince William Sound. This narrow spine of the Chugach Mountains is all that connects the Kenai to the rest of Alaska.

Summit Lake, Chugach National Forest.

The British explorer Captain Cook sailed the waters surrounding the Kenai in 1778, searching for the fabled Northwest Passage. After several dead ends, he explored one promising inlet, but it narrowed, grew shallower, and finally ended. He was forced to turn back again. Cook named this channel the "River Turnagain." Known today as Turnagain Arm, the channel is the eastern extension of Cook Inlet and forms the northern border of the Kenai Peninsula.

These turbulent waters are stirred by some of the largest tides in the world. Whirlpools, breaking waves, and violent tide rips occur as the sea rushes out, exposing broad mud flats. The incoming surge of a thirty-foot tide can build up a steep wall of foaming water known as a bore tide. Although boaters steer clear of Turnagain Arm, adventurous windsurfers find these waters a thrilling challenge.

Remnants of the huge glacier that carved Turnagain Arm still exist in the Chugach Mountains. One of these remnants is arguably the most famous glacier in the world—over half a million people visit it annually. Portage Glacier lies just fifty-five miles from Anchorage at the north end of the Kenai Peninsula.

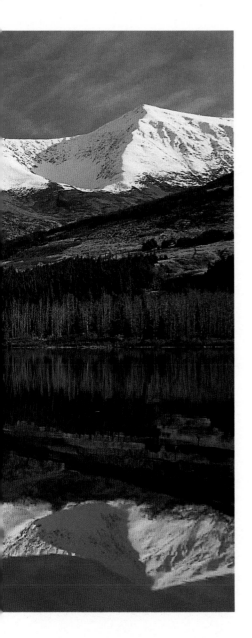

A view of iceberg-filled Portage Lake from the Begich-Boggs Visitor Center.

Page 8: Turnagain Arm.
Page 9: Ice cave in Kenai Fjords National Park.

This river of hard blue ice creeps down the valley at an average rate of a foot per day. It melts and breaks up, though, faster than the ice field above can feed it. Slowly, it is growing shorter, retreating back into the mountains where it was born. In its wake is the sparkling Portage Lake, over 600 feet deep and filled with dazzling blue icebergs. They float, shift, and roll as if performing some slow-motion dance, eventually melting and running into the sea.

Portage Valley is just one small part of the vast Chugach National Forest, the second largest national forest in the United States. It dominates the northeastern portion of the Kenai Peninsula. The Seward Highway winds through the forest past stands of spruce, birch, and hemlock. Gold-bearing streams pour from the high country. Jagged peaks reach for the sky. A carpet of alpine tundra spreads above tree line. Snow free for only a few months each year, the high country bursts with colorful wildflowers in the long summer light. In the fall, the foliage turns vibrant shades of red, gold, and orange—a final blaze of glory before the snow flies and the silence of the long Alaskan winter descends upon the land.

Mountain range in the Chugach National Forest.

GLACIERS

Portage Glacier.

Thousands of tons of cold blue ice—scraping, gouging, and changing the land. Movers of mountains, shapers of landscapes, and awesome reminders of ages past, glaciers are among the most mysterious, beautiful, and powerful agents of geological change on earth. They display a frightening sort of beauty and are at once massive, chaotic, and utterly beyond our control. Glaciers dominate their surroundings.

On Alaska's Kenai Peninsula, nearly 1,800 square miles, or roughly 11 percent, of the peninsula is covered with ice. From narrow, ice-choked fjords to wide, flat-bottomed river valleys, from sheer alpine amphitheaters to flat lands pocked with lakes and ponds, the glaciers of the Kenai have been and continue to be a major force in determining the shape, feel, and appearance of this land.

Glaciers can exist anywhere the annual snowfall is consistently greater than the annual snow melt. As years go by, "leftover" snow piles higher and higher. Deep within this pile, snow is slowly changed into ice through a combination of melting, refreezing, and pressure. This pressure, combined with the force of gravity, causes the ice to flow downhill like a slow, giant river. Glaciers patiently plow through mountain valleys, moving tons of rock with them.

The glaciers of the Kenai Peninsula come in all shapes and sizes, from small, unnamed chunks of fractured ice clinging to high ridges to the gracefully curving ten-mile-long Bear Glacier. Some, like Exit Glacier, end on rocky, flat plains, while others, like Holgate Glacier, flow to tide-water where they calve, or break off, enormous icebergs into narrow ocean fjords. They are fed by the frequent storms born in the Gulf of Alaska, which dump forty to eighty feet of snow a year on the Kenai Mountains. Glaciers have existed here for hundreds of thousands of years and are an integral part of the Kenai—dynamic, unhurried, relentless agents of change, beauty, and mystery.

CHAPTER 2

SOUTHEASTERN PENINSULA

"Sourdough" is what they used to call old-timers in Alaska—those early miners and fur traders

toughened by years of surviving in the harsh north country. Legend has it that two sourdoughs were

enjoying a drink in the young town of Seward when an argument began. It was not a heated argument,

but rather a gentlemanly disagreement that ended in a friendly wager: Could a man run to the top of

Mt. Marathon and back in less than an hour? The year was 1909 and thus Alaska's oldest organized

footrace was born.

Mt. Marathon.

Runners descending the base of
Mt. Marathon in the annual
Fourth of July race.

Page 14: Mt. Alice, near Seward.
Page 15: Devil's club.

Each Fourth of July, nearly 500 participants dash up Mt. Marathon to the 3,022-foot turnaround point and then slip, slide, and stumble their way back down into Seward. Although the first winner required more than an hour to complete the course in 1915, today it is done in less. The runners have been called brave, foolish, and even crazy. Thousands of spectators line the streets of Seward to cheer them on.

The city of Seward lies nestled between rugged peaks at the head of glacier-carved Resurrection Bay. Named for William H. Seward, the U.S. Secretary of State who arranged the purchase of Alaska from the Russians, the town site was chosen in 1902 by surveyors for the Alaska Railroad. They were seeking a deep-water port that could connect the shipping routes with rail lines to the Interior. Seward became a supply center and a vital shipping link. For years it was known as the "Gateway to Alaska."

If Mt. Marathon is what puts Seward on the map for one day each summer, then Kenai Fjords National Park is a major reason it is famous the rest of the season. Seward is the starting point for exploring this splendid, sparkling gem of

A tranquil alpine pond above Beauty Bay, Kenai Fjords National Park.

a park. One of the most beautiful areas in a land characterized by beauty, the park serves as an example of everything Alaska's coasts have to offer—deep, glacier-carved fjords; towering, ragged headlands; booming tidewater glaciers; and varied and abundant marine life.

Entering the fjords is like entering a dream world. It seems more like a fantasy than real life—the product of some wild imagination. On these rocky headlands are written the stories of a thousand winter storms. In these steep fjords are carved the sculptures of ice ages past. Glaciers still thunder here. Whales spout and leap among fantastically shaped icebergs. Colorful puffins buzz overhead. Mountain heights soar from a deep green sea. Ocean mists shroud the lush slopes.

Nature's work is unfinished here. In Holgate Arm, visitors witness geology in action. As if in slow motion, tons of ice collapse from the face of Holgate Glacier into the ocean, shattering the silence. A summer rainstorm sets the cliffs alive with scores of waterfalls, slowly washing the mountains into the sea. This is a land dominated by basic forces: wind, water, ice, and rock.

Harding Ice Field.

Just outside of the fjords at the very edge of the stormy Gulf of Alaska lie the Chiswell Islands, which are part of the Alaska Maritime Wildlife Refuge. Seabirds flock here by the hundreds of thousands to nest on the cliffs. Below the noisy rookeries, Steller sea lions sun themselves on rocky haul outs, or resting places, worn smooth by generations of blubbery sea lion flesh.

Crowning the park and feeding such glaciers as Holgate, Aialik, and Bear is the 300-square-mile Harding Ice Field. The ice age is not quite over in this corner of the world. All but the highest peaks are buried by a vast, unbroken plain of snow and ice. Like a giant collecting pool, the delicate snowflakes of year after year accumulate here. Slowly the snow is converted into hard, blue glacial ice, which flows downhill where it eventually shatters, melts, and runs toward the sea.

Just north of Seward, Exit Glacier flows three miles from the Harding Ice Field to end on flat, gravelly plain. This is the only part of Kenai Fjords National Park accessible by car. In fact, Exit Glacier is perhaps the most accessible glacier in all of Alaska. Here you can walk right up and stare the ice age in the face. Towering cliffs of jagged blue ice rise hundreds of feet above the valley floor. The magnitude and power of the glacier is difficult to comprehend. It appears to be the work of a sculptor completely ignorant of human scale. Like much of Alaska, Exit Glacier can leave you feeling dwarfed by the sheer scope of the landscape.

Three Hole Point in Aialik Bay, Kenai Fjords National Park.

Exit Glacier.

Stormy skies over Kenai Fjords National Park.

Sonny Fox Mine, Kenai Fjords National Park.

Black bear.

WILDLIFE

It is a wild place. Moose roam the woodlands in abundance. Elusive wolves and brown bears slip through the underbrush. Caribou, Dall sheep, and mountain goats graze the high country. River otters and beavers ply the many waterways, while minks, martens, and weasels roam forest floors in search of their dinner. Goshawks dart through the cool spruce forests while the mysterious lynx silently stalks its prey. Bald eagles intently watch as black bears comb the beaches for carrion.

Offshore, sea otters dive and play as pods of whales return from distant wintering grounds. Sea lions bellow from rocky haul outs, or resting places, while birds gather by the thousands to breed and raise their young. The drama of predator and prey, the pulse of seasonal abundance and want—all part of the natural cycle of untamed life on the Kenai Peninsula.

Moose are by far the most common large mammal here; an estimated 8,000 wander the Kenai. They often remain hidden, though, deep within the scrubby thickets of young willow and birch that sustain them. An early morning or late evening drive is the best bet for spotting a cow and calf browsing twigs along the roadside or a lone bull wading chest deep in a pond, searching for water lily roots.

More frequently seen are the dwellers of exposed cliffs and open mountain meadows—the Dall sheep and mountain goats of the Kenai Mountains. Bands of wild Dall rams roam the windswept ridges, sporting magnificent curled horns and occasionally clashing heads with rival males in displays of dominance. The ewes and lambs form their own groups and peacefully feed on grasses.

Mountain goats, with their short, black horns and shaggy coats, inhabit some of the steepest, most extreme terrain of any animal in Alaska. The Exit Glacier area of Kenai Fjords National Park is an excellent place to spot solitary billies or gregarious nannies and kids traversing the precipitous heights.

Bull moose.

Humpback whale.

Respected by animal and human alike, the brown bear also calls the Kenai home. A noted Alaska game biologist, when asked which parts of the peninsula brown bears occupy, responded, "They occupy anything they want to." They are truly the kings of the forest. More than any other creature, the brown bear represents the power, beauty, and unpredictability of the untamed Alaskan wilderness.

Its smaller cousin, the black bear, is more widespread and common. Curious and often unafraid, black bears have been spotted lumbering across glaciers, snoozing beneath parked cars, swimming in ice-filled fjords, and even sunning themselves on beaches. Although usually wary of humans, the black bear is the bear most likely to turn up in backyards and campsites looking for an easy meal.

The rich ocean waters surrounding the Kenai are home to a tremendous variety of marine life. White beluga whales surface and disappear in the murky waters of Cook Inlet like ghostly apparitions. Huge schools of salmon appear each summer and fall as if by magic. Mighty sea lion bulls, wearing scars inflicted by their rivals, nervously patrol the beaches while guarding their harems.

Long hours of sunlight encourage the growth of tiny algae and plankton during the summer months, making these waters among the richest feeding grounds in the world. Humpback whales travel hundreds of miles to raise their young in the deep, cold fjords edging the Gulf of Alaska. Sea birds gather by the hundreds of thousands on ancestral breeding grounds to hatch and feed their chicks. Colorful puffins splash at the ocean surface, so bloated with fish they cannot fly. Kittiwakes wheel and dive in the cold sea breezes. The rhythm of life, untamed and free, goes on here as it has forever.

Steller sea lions.

Overlooking Seward and Resurrection Bay from Mt. Marathon.

The cliffs of Kenai Fjords National Park come alive with cascading waterfalls in springtime.

Morning mist lingers over dead stands of spruce near Beauty Bay. The 1964 Anchorage earthquake dropped the Kenai coast six to eight feet, allowing salt water to encroach upon the land, killing the forests.

EARTHQUAKE!

*The 1964 earthquake caused massive damage as this aerial view of Seward shows.
Some scientists say the 8.6 Richter-scale measurement is too conservative.*

The heavy ski boots beat a staccato roll as the young girl rushed with her brothers and sister down six flights of ancient wooden stairs. From the door of an old mine building located high in the mountains, the children burst out into the snowy parking lot as the earth trembled on . . . and on . . . and on. The bulldozer used for clearing snow from the road jumped about like popcorn in a hot skillet. Avalanches poured down every gully and steep slope around the basin as the shaking gradually subsided. Slowly, the snow clouds settled while the last of the sunlight faded from the towering peaks.

The Mitchells were one of several families that had traveled to Independence Mine for a long Easter weekend of spring skiing, never expecting their plans to be disrupted by a massive earthquake. After the shaking stopped—in what had seemed like an eternity to young Sarah Mitchell—the somber parents and subdued children located each other in the growing dusk.

The families gathered in front of the roaring fire in the old mine superintendent's house to listen to the radio reports. The crackle of burning spruce in the fireplace punctuated the radio static while speculation and questions circled among the group. After an hour, the local station finally came on the air with sobering news of the damage and issued emergency directions and personal messages to family and loved ones.

As strong aftershocks continued into the night, the stranded families stayed glued to the radio—their only link to the outside world. They learned that others had not been as lucky. The powerful aftershocks shook broken buildings off slump blocks, and tidal waves swept ashore as residents of coastal towns fled into the hills. Some even resorted to climbing tall trees in a last-ditch effort to find safety.

The following morning, southcentral Alaska rose to its feet. People began digging out belongings from fractured houses and started rebuilding roads and homes and towns.

Tidal waves crowned with burning fuel had swept into Seward and demolished the small boat harbor and docks. The frozen land cracked as it settled, splitting trees and houses. Glacial clay liquefied and ran into the sea, and then the tide turned and carried the clay back into sunken forests and houses.

For the families still trapped at Independence Mine, the wait to travel down the mountain had just begun. The mine road was choked by a dozen avalanches and the bridges over the major rivers had tumbled off their pilings. The large bulldozer—undamaged after having been tossed around as if several tons of steel weighed nothing—was put to work pushing a one-lane road through the masses of earth and snow left by the avalanches. Rickety bridges were hastily built across the Matanuska and Knik rivers.

Four days after the earthquake, the Mitchell family was finally able to drive to Anchorage where they abandoned their car and flew home to the Kenai. Greeted by their terrified cats, the Mitchells thankfully discovered that their homestead had escaped with minor damage. As happy as Sarah was to be home at last, she knew there was a lot of work to be done to put the place in order again. And in the end, the massive job of restacking ten cords of firewood and a six-month supply of canned goods was assigned to—just as Sarah knew it would be—the kids.

CHAPTER 3

CENTRAL PENINSULA

Great sheets of ice once reigned here. They pushed up piles of rock, which today are tree-covered hills. They carved shallow basins, which are now wetlands dotted with ponds. They gouged deep troughs, which today are lakes rich with fish. Times change. What was once a desert of ice is now lowland forest teeming with life—placid lakes graced with white swans, the voice of a loon rising in the dawn, and sparkling rivers flowing wild and free.

Fishing buoys decorate the fence surrounding a log house in Kenai.

Kelly Lake, Kenai National Wildlife Refuge.

Anglers crowd the banks of the Kenai River to take part in "combat fishing."

Page 28: A beaver pond in the Chugach Mountains, Kenai National Wildlife Refuge.

Page 29: Cranberries and lichens.

The central Kenai Peninsula is dominated by the Kenai National Wildlife Refuge. This vast wilderness reserve covers nearly two million acres, or about one third of the entire Kenai Peninsula. Originally established in 1941 to protect the large moose population, the refuge is also home to brown and black bears, Dall sheep, mountain goats, caribou, and wolves among other animals. It stretches from the 6,612-foot summit of Truuli Peak, the highest point on the peninsula, to the mud flats of Cook Inlet. The refuge has been called a "miniature Alaska" because it contains most habitat types found in the state. These habitats include wetlands, forest, tundra, and mountains.

This area is an important Alaskan playground for residents and visitors alike. Hunters, hikers, and photographers can explore the lowlands and hills on approximately fifty miles of trails. Each summer, hundreds of adventurers travel the 150 miles of the Swanson and Swan rivers canoe system. They paddle by stands of spindly black spruce, beside loons with newly hatched chicks, beneath ravens soaring on afternoon breezes, near beavers building jumbled dams, or perhaps past a newborn moose calf testing its shaky legs.

Including the Swanson, nine river systems drain the refuge, providing spawning grounds for five species of Alaskan salmon: kings, reds, pinks, silvers, and chum, or dog salmon. It is estimated that 40 percent of Cook Inlet's commer-

cial fishing industry is supported directly by refuge-spawned fish.

The waters of the central peninsula also support a thriving sport fishery. Red salmon return to the Russian River by the hundreds of thousands during June and July. Monstrous king salmon, weighing up to 100 pounds, migrate up the Kenai River each spring and summer. Anglers come from around the world to try their luck in these prolific rivers. At the peak of the salmon runs, fishers line the banks shoulder to shoulder in a yearly Alaskan ritual known as "combat fishing."

The Kenai River drains from the spectacular Kenai Lake. Filling a long, glacier-carved trough, the lake is fed by streams that drain the Kenai Mountains, many of which originate at glaciers. These glaciers grind and pulverize rock as they flow downhill. This rock flour, or silt, is carried by the streams to Kenai Lake. There, the tiny silt particles are suspended in the water, refracting the light and lending the lake a beautiful greenish turquoise color.

Many people access the Kenai River and its world-class fishing from the city of Soldotna. This is modern Alaska. Soldotna did not even exist until the late 1940s when the area was opened to homesteaders. Today, it is the seat of the Kenai Peninsula Borough government and a commercial center for the entire peninsula. People arrive from hours away to visit their dentist, buy a new car, or indulge in fast food in Soldotna.

Bald eagle.

Just ten miles from Soldotna, the Kenai River empties into Cook Inlet. Here, at its mouth, Athabaskan Indians thrived for thousands of years. In the eighteenth century, Russian fur traders chose this location to build Fort St. Nicholas. Today, the city of Kenai sits on the bluffs overlooking Cook Inlet. It is the largest city on the peninsula and an industrial and commercial fishing center. Industry thrives in Kenai thanks to the discovery of oil in 1957. Over half of Kenai's residents are employed by oil-related businesses. There are offshore drilling rigs, chemical plants, and oil refineries nearby.

Despite the development, nature is still close at hand. Beluga whales enter the mouth of the river during the summer in pursuit of fish. On a clear day, the steam from the great volcanoes of the Aleutian Range is visible across Cook Inlet. Caribou are seen grazing from the road on the Kenai River flats. Hundreds of snow geese join them there during spring and fall migrations. Wild Alaska is never far away on the Kenai Peninsula.

Evening light at Kenai Lake, Chugach National Forest.

OIL

Oil tanker anchored in Kachemak Bay.

Oil was discovered on the Kenai Peninsula in July 1957 near the Swanson River in the Kenai National Wildlife Refuge. The discovery launched the equivalent of a modern-day gold rush to the peninsula and elsewhere in Alaska. The generation of wealth that followed propelled Alaska to statehood in 1958, helped to found and fund the new state, and led to the eventual discovery of oil in Prudhoe Bay in 1968.

In the years between 1959 and 1991, eight oil fields and twenty-three gas fields on the Kenai Peninsula and in Cook Inlet produced a combined total of 1.1 billion barrels of oil and over 65 trillion cubic feet of gas. The extraction and manufacturing of oil and gas, as well as the many businesses servicing these industries, now account for an estimated 36 to 42 percent of total employment on the Kenai Peninsula.

In 1989, the bill for all this wealth came due. Early in the morning on March 24, the colossal supertanker Exxon *Valdez*, carrying Prudhoe Bay crude oil from the pipeline terminal in Valdez, ran aground on the rocks of Bligh Reef.

The supertanker gushed almost 11 million gallons of lethal crude into Prince William Sound.

But the damage did not stop there—the deadly oil slick traveled hundreds of miles, fouling the coastlines of the Chugach National Forest; the Alaska Maritime, Kodiak, and Alaska Peninsula/Becharof national wildlife refuges; the Kenai Fjords and Katmai national parks; and the Aniakchak National Monument and Preserve. In its wake lay the corpses of hundreds of thousands of birds, sea otters, and harbor seals. The toll on habitats, subsistence resources, and areas heretofore considered benchmarks of environmental purity may never be accurately tabulated.

An Exxon official stated in an October 1992 letter to *Time* magazine that "in the long term the environment does come back." Indeed, for many, the spill may be just a distant memory. But for the Alaskans who lived the Exxon *Valdez* oil spill—the clean-up workers, the wildlife retrieval crews, the anguished land managers, the fishers and Native people whose livelihood vanished—the destruction will never be forgotten.

Skiing near Turnagain Arm.

SPORTS & ACTIVITIES

Rural Alaskans often comment, "Anchorage is a real nice place. It's the closest city to Alaska." The Alaska they refer to is the Kenai—backyard and playground for southcentral Alaskan residents and visitors alike. For many visitors, the primary destinations are Portage Glacier and Seward, which is the gateway to Kenai Fjords National Park. The fifty-five-mile drive from Anchorage to Portage Glacier can turn into an afternoon's adventure with frequent stops along the Seward Highway to discover the beauty of Turnagain Arm.

At Turnagain Arm, take the opportunity to marvel at the windsurfers skimming over the whitecaps, to photograph the ever-changing light and shadows drifting across the Kenai Mountains, or to watch a passing pod of silvery beluga whales following migrating salmon. One unique characteristic of this area is the three-foot tidal bore that surges into Turnagain Arm at twenty miles per hour. It is best to watch the tide from a distance, however, because although the tidal flats may look inviting, especially when covered with bright purple lupine, they are dangerous to walk on. The tidal flats are composed of a gray-colored clay that acts like quicksand, which, combined with the fast-moving tide, can be a deadly combination.

Upon arriving at Portage Glacier, located at the east end of Turnagain Arm, stormy weather often dictates an indoor tour of the visitor center, where one can see towering icebergs rising up from Portage Lake. If weather permits, a hike to Byron Glacier or a voyage on the MV *Ptarmigan* is the best way to get a closer look at Portage Glacier.

For adventurous travelers who yearn to try something new, a train ride to Whittier, the entrance to Prince William Sound, is a fun side trip. But this is no ordinary journey—cars and motor homes can be driven right onto the train at Portage for a thirty-minute ride through the tunnels and scenic valleys. Once in Whittier, charter a boat, ride the ferry, or paddle your own sea kayak to explore the intricate waterways of the Kenai's eastern coast.

After returning to Portage, follow the Seward Highway into the Kenai Mountains. Turnagain Pass is a principle winter playground for skiers and snowmobilers. Snowmobilers race on the west side of the pass, while backcountry skiers tour the valleys and slopes of the east side. Hikers can follow the Resurrection Pass trail system, which is about sixty-five miles long and stretches from near Hope to Cooper Landing and on to Exit Glacier near Seward. The trails are dotted with public-use cabins every six to ten miles. Reservations can be made through the Forest Service to ensure a warm and dry place to stay on stormy nights.

The town of Seward, situated at the head of Resurrec-

Climbing in Kenai Fjords National Park.

Canoeing on the upper Kenai River, Chugach National Forest.

tion Bay, marks the beginning of the Seward Highway. Exit Glacier, the most accessible glacier in Kenai Fjords National Park, is just nine miles from the Seward Highway. A rough, steep trail ascends the north side of Exit Glacier to the Harding Ice Field. The trek affords breathtaking views of Harding Ice field, Exit Glacier, and the valley below—but the trail is for experienced hikers only. To see another side of Kenai Fjords National Park, explore the rugged coast by boat. Companies based in Seward offer chartered boat tours of the park and the coastal islands of the Alaska Maritime National Wildlife Refuge. Since cold weather and windy conditions prevail throughout the year, it is recommended that warm clothes and rain gear be worn on the tours.

The Kenai abounds with fishing opportunities throughout the year. Sport becomes social during the red salmon run as anglers crowd shoulder to shoulder on the banks of the Kenai River. Fishing derbies are held throughout the summer in coastal communities like Homer, which is considered the capital of Pacific halibut sportfishing. High-stakes prizes go to anglers who catch large or specially tagged fish.

For extended fishing trips—as well as hiking, boating, climbing, and skiing trips—there are a number of campsites along the Seward and Sterling highways in the Chugach National Forest. Several state recreation areas, including Caines Head, Captain Cook, and Clam Gulch state recreation areas also have campsites. Camping is permitted throughout most of the Kenai National Wildlife Refuge, and visitors are welcome to pitch a tent on the Homer Spit. A trip down the Sterling Highway to the scenic town of Homer is well worth the drive.

Whether river rafting down the Kenai River or scaling a snow-covered peak, one can feel the inexplicable beauty of a wild place where nature is close at hand. If we are to preserve this wilderness for generations to come, then we must leave no mark upon the land. For today, all we take are memories—of good times and adventures—and the promise of tomorrow's travels.

Windsurfing in Turnagain Arm.

Cotton grass seeds bloom along Arctic Lake, Kenai National Wildlife Refuge. The lake drained in 1992 and is currently refilling.

NATIVE ALASKANS

Native Alaskans near Seldovia, 1901.

The Dena'ina, or "the people," call the Kenai Peninsula *Yaghanen*, "The Good Land." The Dena'ina are unique among Athabaskan peoples in that they adapted to a marine environment. The abundant marine life, edible plants, and land mammals of the Kenai provided the Dena'ina with a wealth of food resources.

The Dena'ina have inhabited the Kenai Peninsula for over a thousand years, yet little is known of their culture prior to European contact in the late 1700s. Artifacts and cultural refuse are surprisingly absent from Dena'ina sites. Were it not for the hundreds of house depressions that dot their prime hunting, fishing, and gathering locations, there would be no record of prehistoric Dena'ina culture.

Modern descendants of the Dena'ina, many of whom belong to the Kenaitze Indian Tribe, continue to live in the same areas inhabited by their ancestors. The city of Kenai, located at the mouth of the Kenai River, was once the site of a main Dena'ina village. The influence of the Russian fur traders and Orthodox priests is still evident today in the architecture of the buildings and other structures in the historic district of Old Towne Kenai.

Although the contemporary Dena'ina are influenced by both the Russian and American cultures, traditional values are important as well. These values are revealed through the *sudku*, or stories, preserved by Native elders such as the writer Peter Kalifornsky of Kenai and the late storyteller Shem Pete of Tyonek.

The stories reflect a deep commitment to conserving the land, plant, and animal resources. The Dena'ina believed that to ensure the continued presence of fish and other animals on which they depended for survival, the animals' bones must be returned to water or burned. The practice of this belief was confirmed by archaeologists when excavated hearths showed high concentrations of burned animal remains.

Like the Dena'ina before them, modern-day residents of the Kenai Peninsula live, work, hunt, and fish in the same places that people have used for thousands of years. The legacy of the Dena'ina is a profound awareness of humankind's tie to the land, which reflects our dependence on its abundant resources and our responsibility to preserve "The Good Land."

CHAPTER 4

SOUTHERN PENINSULA

Perhaps the only thing more diverse than the inhabitants of the southern Kenai Peninsula is the land itself. Glaciers, wind, water, earthquakes, and volcanic ash have all left their mark on this land. From the rolling forested hills and muskegs, or mossy bogs, of Clam Gulch south to Kachemak Bay and beyond, the Kenai Mountains rise above fjords and forests to dominate the landscape.

A perch atop East Hill affords a panoramic view of Homer, Kachemak Bay, and the snow-covered Kenai Mountains.

Along Cook Inlet, the shoreline between Clam Gulch and Anchor Point provides outdoor enthusiasts with a playground for fishing, clamming, and sightseeing. Miles of clam beaches are available to the determined many who do not mind digging up to their elbows in sand for the delicious razor clams. Looking for a catch of a different sort, anglers flock to Ninilchik River, Deep Creek, Anchor River, and Cook Inlet to cast or troll for fighting salmon, steelhead, trout, and halibut. For those interested in scenic beauty, an especially picturesque spot is the Ninilchik hilltop where the historic Russian Orthodox church is framed by the mountains rising in the distance across Cook Inlet. The church's backdrop of mountains, including the four steaming volcanoes Mt. Augustine, Mt. Iliamna, Mt. Redoubt, and Mt. Spurr, is visible from Clam Gulch to Homer.

The city of Homer is located on the north shore of Kachemak Bay "where the land ends and the sea begins." It is both the commercial and cultural center of the southern peninsula. Cresting the Homer bluffs, visitors are treated to a

Homer Harbor.

Fishermen proudly display their day's catch of salmon and halibut.

Page 38: Mt. Augustine, an active volcano, looms up in the waters of Cook Inlet.

Page 39: Jellyfish and marine algae.

view of the majestic panorama of snow-covered mountains and the Homer Spit snaking out into Kachemak Bay. This bay is one of the richest marine environments in the world. It yields barn-door size halibut and all five species of Pacific salmon for sport fishers. The bay also supports a commercial fishery for salmon, halibut, bottom fish, and crab and provides an outdoor laboratory for coastal study. In this pristine natural setting, visitors can marvel at raucous seabird rookeries dotted with colorful puffins; observe whales, seals, and otters from kayaks or tour boats; and comb the beach for unusual tide-pool creatures.

An intriguing mix of people have settled to create Homer, this "Cosmic Hamlet by the Sea." Homer was originally founded in the late 1800s by coal miners and gold seekers, who were followed by commercial fishers and home-steaders. More recent inhabitants in the area include the Russian Old Believers, who have created several settlements near Homer and in the Fox River Valley. The Homerites' spirited sense of community is evident in the friendly hellos and in the expression of strong—and widely diverse—opinions on many topics.

The Kenai Mountains are a majestic backdrop for these horseback riders on Homer Spit.

Artists and writers find a welcoming haven in Homer's laid-back atmosphere. Art galleries are filled with original paintings, pottery, fiber arts, sculpture, photographs, and jewelry. Visitors can enjoy community theater and concerts or join the locals at the Salty Dawg Saloon, where sawdust covers the floor, creating a nostalgic atmosphere. They can also tour the fascinating Pratt Museum, which is nationally recognized for its oil-spill exhibit. A stop at the Alaska Maritime National Wildlife Refuge visitor center provides information about the marine wildlife viewing and natural history in Kachemak Bay and on coastlines throughout Alaska. Homer is also a land and sea transportation center for commercial shipping and for booking charters to the small communities, wilderness lodges, and state parks on the south shore of Kachemak Bay.

Kachemak Bay State Park and Kachemak Bay State Wilderness Park are majestic road-free wilderness characterized by towering ancient spruce forests, misty fjords, rugged peaks, and massive glaciers. This untamed land is an adventurer's paradise. Explore the trails on a day hike or backpack on an extended trip; soar in a floatplane over the moss-laden rain forest to fish in a remote mountain lake; glide by sea kayak to view the rookeries of marine mammals and sea birds; hunt for mountain goats, bear, and moose; or gather your dinner from fertile beaches, berry-covered slopes, or salmon-filled rivers.

Halibut Cove, Kachemak Bay State Park.

From Clam Gulch, Mt. Iliamna and Mt. Redoubt volcanoes appear in silhouette across Cook Inlet.

Mystery still shrouds the unwritten history of the Pacific Eskimos and Dena'ina Indians, who lived on the southern shore of Kachemak Bay for many centuries before Russian traders arrived in the late 1700s. The Native people are now centered in Seldovia, Nanwalek (formerly English Bay), and Port Graham, all of which are accessible only by air or sea. While Nanwalek and Port Graham remain remote—thriving through commercial fishing, Native corporation investments, and by gathering subsistence foods—Seldovia has grown substantially with white settlers and has frequent air and water ferry service.

Also located on the south shore of Kachemak Bay is the picturesque fishing village of Halibut Cove, with its art galleries and seaside houses built on pilings. The people of Halibut Cove rely on the fishing, wildlife, and other natural resources of the Kachemak Bay region, as have all of the Kachemak Bay communities since aboriginal times. Coping with the Alaskan weather, extended periods of darkness, expensive transportation of goods, and fluctuations in the Alaskan economy have strengthened these enterprising people. They display an individualistic, pioneering spirit typical of the Kenai Peninsula.

RUSSIAN OLD BELIEVERS

Young women with a bucket of freshly gathered mushrooms.

Russian Old Believers first came to Alaska in 1967 seeking an "island of faith" where they could live peacefully and practice the tenets of pre-Nikonian Orthodoxy. Their refusal to follow the doctrinal changes demanded by Patriarch Nikon in 1654 resulted in excommunication, exile, and persecution for the next 275 years. Millions of Old Believers were executed in the years prior to their exodus to other countries following the Communist revolution. Their long search for religious freedom eventually lead them to Alaska's Kenai Peninsula where they built the community of Nikolaevsk.

Just a generation ago, Nikolaevsk was a dream—a vision in the mind's eye of those who would preserve the traditions, beliefs, and values of old Russia. Its miraculous birth in a remote Kenai Peninsula spruce forest on December 19, 1968, was accompanied by the scream of chain saws and the prayers of bearded men. The saws are rarely heard today but prayers continue to accompany every element of the small community's growth.

After generations of persecution, the Old Believers have finally found a home. Nikolaevsk is a little taste of Russia—a microcosm of prerevolutionary Russia planted in Alaskan soil. The picturesque houses with their intricate woodwork and icons over the doors, the women in bright dresses and scarves, the bearded men in embroidered shirts and belts, and the children wearing traditional hairstyles are all reminiscent of *Fiddler on the Roof*. The seventeenth-century Russian spoken by the more than three hundred residents further confirms the Old Believers' adherence to traditional ways.

Russian Orthodox church, Ninilchik.

*Icicles frame a young Native boy taking a
respite from a January cold spell.*

Seldovia Harbor.

Page 48: Dog mushing beneath a canopy of snow-covered alder.